GET OUTDOORS

Canoeing and Kayaking

Lois Rock

WAYLAND

First published in 2008 by Wayland

Copyright © Wayland 2008

Wayland
338 Euston Road
London NW1 3BH

Wayland Australia
Level 17/207 Kent Street
Sydney NSW 2000

Senior editor: Jennifer Schofield
Designer: Rachel Hamdi and Holly Fulbrook
Photographer: John Cleare – www.mountaincamera.com
Photoshoot co-ordinator: Rita Storey

Acknowledgements:
The author and publisher would like to thank the following people for participating in our photoshoot: Kendal Bromley-Bewes, Susie Corkery, Leander Crocker-Digby, Grace Earley, Ben Hedden, Alice Shoulder and George Shoulder.

A special thank you to Michel Bewsey at www.aswatersports.co.uk for supplying the equipment and Ben Hedden and Suzie Corkery of the Haven Banks Outdoor Education Centre for their help and advice.

All photography by John Cleare except
4 Mansell/Time & Life Pictures/Getty Images; 7 bottom Maxim Marmur/AFP/Getty Images; 29 top Doug Pensinger/Getty Images

British Library Cataloguing in Publication Data
Rock, Lois, 1953-
   Canoeing and kayaking. - (Get outdoors)
   1. Canoes and canoeing - Juvenile literature
   I. Title
   797.1'22

ISBN: 978 0 7502 5061 0

Printed in China

Wayland is a division of Hachette Children's Books,
an Hachette Livre UK company.
www.hachettelivre.co.uk

Contents

What are canoe sports?

Canoeing is one of the simplest ways to go boating. You take your place in a boat for one (or two) and use a paddle to propel yourself through the water, facing the direction of travel. You have to spot what is up ahead and choose a course through it. This may be a straightforward route, gliding on calm open water, or a challenging course that twists and turns among rocks and spray. Canoeing is a sport that lets you set yourself a personal challenge and come through grinning.

Open canoes

The so-called open canoe was used by several of the native peoples of North America to travel across the country's many lakes and rivers. The canoes were made from a lightweight wooden frame, covered with birchbark that was laced and glued in place. The paddle was made from wood and its single blade was used skilfully in a variety of strokes. In this way, the paddler could travel silently over long distances. The canoe was an excellent means of transport for people and their belongings.

The traditional paddling position is kneeling. Modern boats usually have seats, but kneeling gives better control.

Kayak

The kayak was the hunting boat of the Inuit people of the Arctic regions. It was made from a simple wooden frame, covered with animal skin. The kayaker used a paddle with a narrow blade at either end, pulling each through the water in turn, to travel through the icy sea in search of prey. On the covered deck, the hunter would have a harpoon for catching seals and a spare single-bladed paddle. This paddle was used in a crisis situation: with a sweep of the blade, a paddler could roll his capsized kayak the right way up.

Canoe or Kayak?

There are so many styles of the modern boat that only one true difference can be named: a canoe is powered with a single-bladed paddle while a kayak is powered with a double-bladed paddle. The so-called C-boat looks very much like a modern kayak, but is paddled with a single blade like a canoe.

If you learn canoe sports, you will be expected to have a go at paddling both canoe and kayak. Learning both disciplines will help you to understand more about boat control.

Why go paddling?

There's something special about setting yourself afloat on water. You are moving from your natural land habitat into a totally different environment. That means you are going to have to learn new skills.

Physical and mental skills

Of these new skills, some are physical: you will need strength, flexibility, balance and the ability to act quickly as you manoeuvre your boat and paddle. Other skills are mental: you will need to learn to understand what water does, how to assess risk and how to respond to that risk. This will teach you to be safe, independent and self reliant.

Paddling with friends can be a lot of fun.

Just for fun

Canoe sport is something you can enjoy just for fun – for the joy of going out and about with friends, adventuring playfully (yet responsibly) in the water and learning to be at ease in that environment.

Seeing wildlife on river banks is part of the adventure.

Exploring the world

Canoeing is a great way to explore the world. Your watery journeys can take you to some beautiful places. You can paddle very close to creatures that naturally make their home in or near water. You may be paddling close to reeds when a heron flaps its huge wings and takes off with easy strength; a kingfisher may dart past like a blue arrow; out at sea, seals may lift their heads to peer at their visitor.

Going for gold

Canoeing also offers a range of sporting opportunities, with its own competition structure. There are two different Olympic disciplines. One is flatwater racing, which requires strong, fast paddling in a straight line. The other is slalom, which involves taking a kayak or specially adapted canoe – a C-boat – down a whitewater course.

The Australian pair at the Olympics K2 race. Training for competition requires years of disciplined work.

How to get started

Canoeing is categorised as a 'risk' sport – and that is part of the fun – but it must never be undertaken recklessly. Start your canoeing in a responsible way and learn the techniques that will keep you safe on the water.

Not quite the deep end

One place to start canoeing is in a large swimming pool.
Pool kayaks are small, light, and easy to manoeuvre.
The water is warm and clear, and solid ground is never far away.
The supervisor can see easily that everyone is safe. Once you are happy in the pool, you can move on to outdoor venues.

Always pay attention to what you are taught BEFORE you get on the water. Otherwise, you may find yourself 'up the creek without a paddle'.

Getting outdoors

Outdoor centres and canoe clubs usually run beginners' sessions on calm, still water where there is also an easy place to launch the boats and to get out again. The person in charge should hold the proper coaching qualifications, and any helpers should also be training for qualification. In Britain, these qualifications are awarded by the sport's governing body, the British Canoe Union (BCU). In the USA the governing body, American Canoeing Association, regulates the sport, while in Australia the sport is governed by Australian Canoeing.

Get-out plan

Every paddling session needs to have a get-out plan: a way to get everyone off the water and safely back to land in an emergency. Never risk paddling unless you are properly supervised. On the water, you need to be sure there is someone out there with you who can help you at once if you find yourself in difficulty.

This paddler has been thrown a bag of rope, with the end held secure by a rescuer on the bank. The paddler grabs the throwline, turns on her back, and is pulled in.

Equipment

Canoeing is boating at its simplest. You will need some equipment, but you can usually begin by borrowing the specialised gear from the centre where you learn your skills. As you begin to make the sport your own, you can buy what you need a piece at a time.

Paddle – you need a paddle that is the right size for your height and light enough for you to handle easily. Kayak paddles are made from lightweight synthetic materials; canoe paddles may be synthetic but wood is the material most paddlers prefer. If you really want to invest in canoeing, a lightweight paddle that is just right for you is an excellent first purchase.

Boat – to go canoeing, you must have a boat. Beginners need a tough, go-anywhere model. The typical all-purpose kayak is made from moulded plastic. A robust modern canoe is made from a layered composite.

Rope – a 'throwbag' of rope is useful safety equipment. You need to learn how to use it safely.

Helmet – this is recommended for beginners and is essential for anyone who paddles in fast water or in rocky places on rivers or seas. A bang to the head could cause a serious injury but might only slightly scratch a helmet.

Buoyancy aid – it is very important to wear a buoyancy aid when canoeing. It will hold you afloat in the water if you take a tumble and leaves you free to clamber to safety. It will also protect your body – against branches, for example.

When it is warm and sunny, canoeists need clothing that protects their skin from sunburn. They also need sunglasses to shield their eyes from the glare off the water.

Spraydeck – this is worn by kayakers to keep water out of their boat. It fits snugly around the waist like a skirt, and the edges grip around the edge of the cockpit in which the paddler sits. You can learn the basics of kayaking without one, but you will learn both how to wear one and how to remove it quickly as you progress.

When it is cold, canoeists and kayakers needs warm, fleecy underlayers. On top of these go waterproof trousers and a 'cag' with a close-fitting collar and cuffs.

Get ready

Anyone who goes canoeing needs to feel happy both near and in the water. Ideally, you should be able to swim at least 50 metres.

Feeling confident on the water

To become used to being in the water, practise tumbling around in a swimming pool so that you are confident in and under water. This is important for weaker swimmers. Be honest with your instructor about your swimming ability and be sure to say if you have any breathing problems, such as asthma. Toppling into the water when boating is always possible. If a sudden ducking is going to be a problem for you, your instructor will want to know and give you closer supervision.

Warm Up

Before any canoeing session it is important to get your muscles moving. Try fast walking, then a short distance of jogging, then fast walking again. Next, practise freestyle swimming movements to loosen your arms and shoulders, or practise your paddle strokes.

Warm down

Canoeing puts stress on your muscles, but this warm down lengthens and relaxes them. Stand tall and imagine two balloons, one tied to each ear, 'lifting' you straight up. Breathe in and hold your tummy tight.

Let your head nod to your chest. Breathing out, let your spine roll down until you are flopped like a rag doll. Then breathe in, tighten your tummy, and breathe out as you roll back up.

Grab a paddle

Choose a shaft that is the right size for your hand. When you paddle kayak, your dominant hand (left or right) stays firm and your other hand lets the shaft roll through the paddle action.

You hold a canoe paddle like this, with one hand covering the grip and the other holding the shaft. You will swap between left and right sides when paddling.

Handle with care

Canoes and kayaks are portable boats, but they are still quite heavy so it is important to learn good lifting techniques. It is best to carry a boat between two people using the grab handles at each end. Bend the knees to reach down for them and keep a straight back.

Check

Before you launch, check the conditions. What is the water like today? What is the wind doing? Are there any hazards – boaters, wildlife or vegetation, for example? Make a note of these things, assess their possible effect on you and adjust your plans to suit.

Launch and land

Getting in and out of your boat is something to practise on land or in shallow, still water. The general rule for launching and getting out on a river is to do so with your boat facing upstream. That way, you can see anything that might be coming down towards you and react.

Kayak launch and landing

1 *Sit on the bank with your paddle where you can grab it. Put your feet in the cockpit of your boat.*

Put your bank-side hand firmly on the back of the boat and grab the outer rim of the cockpit as you pull yourself round. Sit on the back of the cockpit before sliding yourself in and gripping with your knees.

2

Where's the Paddle?

Kayakers should have their paddle on the bank and parallel to their boat, so they can grab it once they are tucked into the boat. Canoeists can lay their paddle in the boat before they step in.

When getting out, keep your weight central as you ease your legs straight and lift yourself out of the cockpit. Then reverse the getting-in instructions. Keep your feet in your boat until you are ready to haul it out.

Canoe launch and landing

The back paddler holds the boat steady while the front paddler steps into the middle and moves forward, paddle at the ready, to hold the boat to the bank.

The front paddler then holds the boat to the bank while the back paddler steps into middle of the canoe and moves back to his or her paddling position. The steps shown here are reversed for getting out.

Sliding a kayak in and out of the water is suitable for lakes and shores. Be careful not to damage the shoreline.

Feel the water

Experienced canoeists understand water. They know how it flows, how it keeps them afloat, and how it interacts with their boat and their paddle. As a learner, it is important to play with different paddle strokes so that you too begin to get that feel. Let yourself enjoy seeing what happens to your boat – even if the result comes as a surprise.

Take charge!

Water is more powerful than any canoeist, but it is predictable. You can use the way it behaves to manouevre your canoe. Act, and water will react.

Pulls and pushes

Your boat will always go in the opposite direction to your paddle action, so practise pushing and pulling the flat of the blade through the water.

Pulling your blade through the water gives you forward power.

Pushing your blade through the water gives reverse power.

Sweeping the flat of your blade in a wide arc gives you turning power. Try forward and reverse sweeps.

Turning strokes

Turning strokes are rarely a problem for beginners – it is going in a straight line that can be the challenge. Experiment with turning by trying to 'draw' a circle round your boat with the blade of the paddle. Try making the turning faster, or slower, or introduce a sudden change of direction. You will soon find you are gaining boat control.

Canoe paddlers do complementary sweeps – one forward, one reverse.

A kayaker holds his elbows high over the paddle when bracing.

Bracing strokes

The principle of bracing strokes is to push down on the water with the flat part of the paddle. The water will resist the paddle, giving the paddler the chance to push him or herself and the boat upright. It takes practice to get the timing right, and getting wet while learning is not unusual!

Get right in!

Canoes and kayaks have a flattish bottom – called the hull – that rounds upwards to the sides. This means the boats are easily manoeuvred in all directions, including upside down! You need to know what to do in case of a sudden capsize. Practise when it is easy and when you can get back to land quickly and get changed.

Kayak capsize drill and rescue

1

Capsized kayakers should bang the upturned hull with their hands to get attention before exiting the boat.

2

Once safely out of the boat, they should try to grab their paddle and the bow of the boat.

3

The rescue boater will tell the swimmer to grab the bow of the rescue boat and help to empty the capsized boat.

4

Once the capsized kayak is empty of water, the rescuer will help the swimmer into the boat.

18

Practise taking off your spraydeck so that you can do it easily in an emergency.

Self rescue

Once you are confident getting out of your boat upside down, you are ready for a spraydeck. It keeps water out of your boat even when the boat is upside down. If you can keep yourself in your kayak with good knee grip, two other rescues become possible.

The Eskimo rescue involves reaching for the bow of your rescue boat from the upside-down position and rolling yourself up.

The Eskimo roll involves using the flat of your paddle in a sweeping arc to make a 'platform' on the water, which you use to roll yourself up.

Kayaks to the Rescue

The rescue techniques used by kayakers make them great for lifeguarding swim events in open water. The swimmers can hang on the back of a kayak and be taken to safety.

19

Full speed ahead

There are many types of canoes and kayaks these days. Some are designed for travelling fast in a straight line, while others are designed for go-anywhere manoeuvrability. Even so, all of them require fine adjustments to your paddle stroke to keep the boat on course. You learn this by experience and one key skill: looking where you want to go.

Forward paddle kayak

A strong forward paddle begins with rotating the whole upper body so you can plant the paddle in the water roughly level with your knees. Unwinding gives whole-body power to the stroke – quite different from relying on arm muscles.

When forward paddling, the blade passes close by the side of the boat.

Forward paddle canoe

As in kayaking, a strong canoe stroke depends on rotating the upper body and planting the blade fully into the water.

Tandem canoe paddlers need to keep their strokes balanced to travel in a straight line.

Rudder control

Rudder strokes use a somewhat trailing paddle to adjust the direction of the boat: the bow tends to turn to mirror the position of the blade. Kayakers can use this technique but, because they are taking strokes on either side with their double paddle, they prefer to keep good direction by fine adjustments to each forward stroke. In canoeing, the stern paddler of a tandem pair or a solo paddler will use ruddering a lot.

The stern paddler can manoeuvre the paddle to rudder the boat and change or correct the direction of travel.

The J-stroke

The J-stroke involves a final rudder twist to a forward stroke of a canoe paddle. It allows the solo canoeist to travel in a straight line while paddling on one side of the boat.

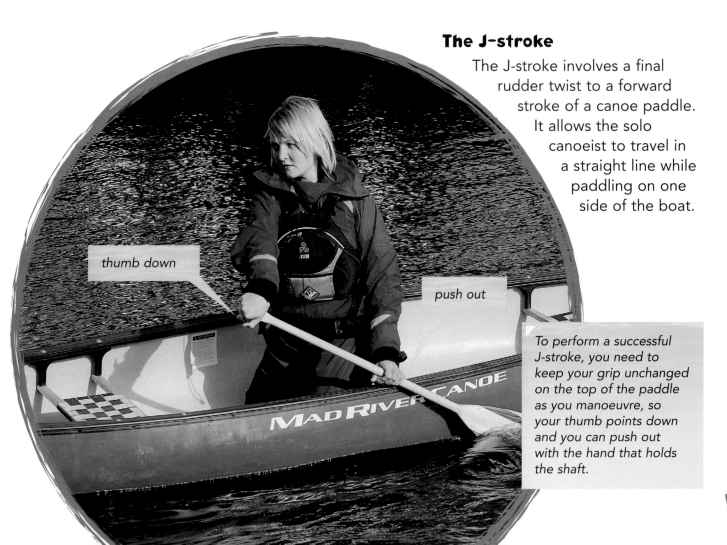

thumb down

push out

To perform a successful J-stroke, you need to keep your grip unchanged on the top of the paddle as you manoeuvre, so your thumb points down and you can push out with the hand that holds the shaft.

Trips and expeditions

When you can manoeuvre your boat and are able to rescue other paddlers and know what to do to be rescued, you can go on trips. For your first expeditions, choose a river that is flat and regularly paddled. Make sure you are allowed to travel it and check with your country's regulatory body for up-to-date information (see page 32).

Kit for a trip

Even a simple trip requires some basic safety kit. It can be kept in a drybag – a waterproof bag with a roll-top closure. A group of paddlers can share the carrying of kit.

A folding paddler's knife to fit in a buoyancy aid is vital for anyone using ropes near water. Ask the advice of a qualified instructor about carrying a knife.

1 A throwbag of rope
2 Extra clothing in case the weather changes
3 Repair tape
4 First aid kit
5 Food and drink
6 Mobile phone/money to make a phone call
7 Sun cream/insect repellent/hand sanitiser
8 Personal medication
9 Spare dry clothing
10 Money for emergencies
11 A heavy-duty karabiner to clip your bag in your boat

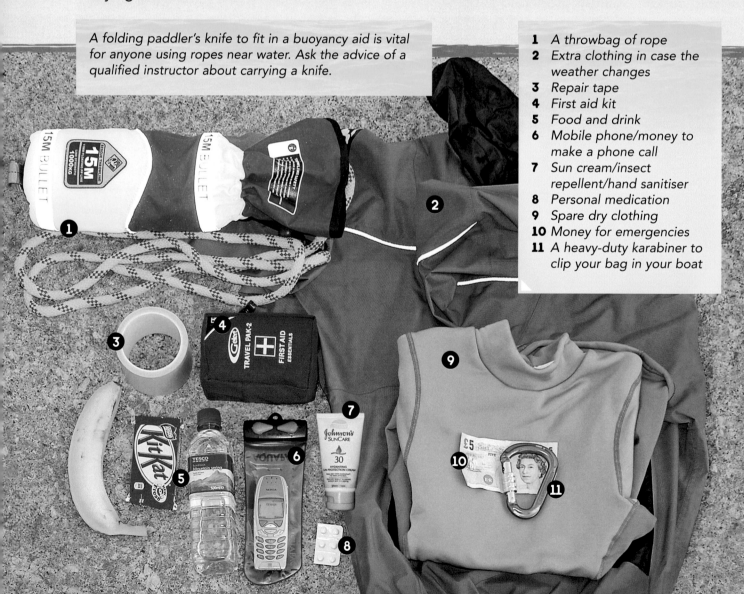

Where are you?

On any trip, you need to be sure there is a responsible adult who can provide back-up. Let him or her know your route and the time you plan to launch and land. You should be able to contact this person easily if you run into problems.

The rule of three

For safety, your trip should include at least three paddlers in three boats. That way, there are two people to help anyone who capsizes. If someone is hurt, one paddler can stay with the person in trouble while the other fetches help. Remember that there should be at least one spare paddle within the group for each sort of boat. Open canoes can easily take spare paddles stashed inside. Kayakers will need splits – paddles that come apart in the middle so that they can be stowed in the stern of a kayak.

Group awareness is key to a happy canoe trip. Stay close enough together for company and safety, so everyone is in sight of at least one other person. Go at the speed of the slowest paddler.

Stay Healthy

Open water is rarely pure. One problem is Weil's disease, which is released in rats' urine. Avoid swallowing any water from an outdoor source and use a hand sanitiser before you eat when you are out paddling. If you feel ill with flu-like symptoms after paddling, see a doctor.

Be a good user

Whenever you are out in your boat, be considerate to other people who are enjoying the water. This includes people on the bank, such as those fishing, as well as other boaters. Remember that it is a privilege to go canoeing. Show respect for the environment – not just the water but also the land, the plants and the wildlife. Be sure to take your litter home with you.

Moving on

As you gain experience, you may be tempted to try faster-flowing rivers. You need to learn how this water works and how to get in and out of the flow safely on so-called 'easy' water – a stretch with very few obstacles and no significant drops.

Grading the Water

There is an international system of grading, from 1 to 6, with grade 1 being the simplest. A majority of whitewater enthusiasts will enjoy paddling up to grades 3 and 4, while 5 and 6 have significant risks.

Flow and eddy

Water always flows downstream. However, wherever there is an obstacle, such as a rock or a jutting-out piece of bank, the water curls back to find its own level behind the obstacle. This curling back creates an eddy. With experience, you can see the change in water pattern between the two: the eddy line.

A kayaker eyes the tiny eddies behind midstream rocks. These eddies show as curling white waves.

Out of the eddy, into the flow

Paddlers usually launch from a bankside eddy. Pointing their boat diagonally upstream, they paddle out into the faster water. This is called breaking in. This catches the bow of the boat and swings it downstream. You will find the trick is to turn your head and body to look eagerly downstream at this moment. This change of position will edge your boat in the downstream direction. If you do not do this the water will catch the upstream edge of the boat and flip you – quickly!

These two canoeists are edging their boat downstream as they paddle out of the bankside eddy. They need to be ready for the sudden turn as the flow catches the bow.

Out of the flow, into the eddy

Paddlers learn to spot eddies – perhaps behind a rock on the side of the river. They must paddle the bow of the boat into the calmer water of the eddy – this is called breakig out. Breaking out stalls the boat, and the stern is swung round by the flow. When you try this manoeuvre, turn your head and body to match the swing and look upstream.

A kayaker is ready with a bracing stroke for the moment her boat leaves the flow for the eddy and swings round its own bow.

Ferry across

It is possible to ferry your boat across a moderate flow of water. To do this, it is vital to edge the boat downstream so that you are paddling diagonally upstream while the flow pushes you back. As a result, you will go straight across.

This kayaker is angling the boat slightly towards the opposite bank as she puts in forward paddle strokes.

Whitewater

Once you are happy on rivers that move along fast but remain largely flat, you can choose to go into water that breaks over drops and obstacles – whitewater. You must learn to assess the risks it presents and know what you can do to deal with them. There will be thrills – and spills.

This pair of paddlers is enjoying the thrill of the whitewater.

New strokes

To run whitewater, you need to find a good line – an imaginary path that avoids obstacles. Look where you are going and use your paddle to go where you want! As you progress, you will learn to link basic strokes in new ways to make other strokes.

When paddling on whitewater, it is especially important to look out for everyone in the group. Everyone should be in the line of sight of at least one other paddler all the time.

Staying safe

Paddling whitewater takes skill and experience, and paddling in the charge of a qualified instructor is the only safe way to learn. Your paddling group should do a risk assessment of the trip. For example, are the paddlers skilful enough for the grade of water? How has recent rainfall affected river levels? There should also be a plan for how to deal with what happens. How will the group stay together on the river? Who will lead and who will be the back marker? What is the strategy for rescuing anyone who takes a tumble? This may be a 'rescue boat' with an experienced paddler who can pick up a swimmer while a 'chase boat' goes after the kit.

If you do not understand the plan or are unhappy with it, speak up before you are committed to paddling. Much more important than any paddling is the life skill of identifying the right choice for you and sticking with your decision.

A world of paddling

When you choose canoeing as your sport, you learn skills that open the ways to the many branches of paddling and that will take you to many different places.

Out to sea

Sea paddling might involve gliding along shining ripples or tossing through a heavy swell. There are many opportunities for organized trips with idyllic scenery and wonderful wildlife that even novice paddlers can enjoy. Those who want to venture out to sea independently need to learn a lot about the patterns of tides and how to cope with wind and waves.

Surfer style

Sea paddling has much in common with board surfing – except that a boat gives more speed to enable the paddler to catch even more waves. Where there is good surf, enthusiasts from other surfing disciplines will want their share of the waves. Kayakers should follow local etiquette about who gives way to whom.

Coastal paddling can be idyllic. However, it is vital to learn about tides and currents before venturing out without a guide.

Freestyle

One of the most popular branches of canoe sport is freestyle. This involves using the power of moving water – and particularly standing waves – to take one's boat through a series of acrobatic manoeuvres.

The great expedition

Whether it is peaceful paddling in perfect places, or a white-knuckle whitewater ride, you can travel by canoe in some of the world's most challenging locations – from seas in Tasmania to Greenland, from North American lakes to the whitewater of Nepal. Then again, there may be great expeditions on water not far from where you live!

This kayaker is perfectly in control, and in the best place in the world – on water!

Glossary

Blade The wide part of a paddle that resists the water.

Bow The nose of a boat.

Brace A stroke that presses the flat of a paddle blade on the water to allow the paddler to keep the boat upright.

Break out The manoeuvre of leaving the flow for an eddy. The manoeuvre from eddying water into the main flow is called breaking in.

Buoyancy aid A sleeveless garment padded with material that floats and will hold a paddler afloat. This is sometimes called a PFD (Personal Flotation Device).

C-boat This boat looks a lot like a modern kayak, but it is manoeuvred with a single bladed paddle, like a canoe.

Cag The name for the waterproof upper garment worn by paddlers. It often has waterproof cuffs and collar.

Capsize Tipping over in a boat.

Cockpit The place in a kayak where the paddler sits.

Deck The upper surface of a kayak.

Downstream A river flows downstream, and faster rivers can be paddled only in this direction.

Drybag A waterproof bag, often with a roll-top closure. Drybags are used to keep kit dry inside a boat.

Eddy The water that swirls back behind an obstacle. Whitewater paddlers typically move from one safe eddy to another.

Ferry A manoeuvre for crossing a river flow without being carried downstream.

Freestyle A branch of canoe sport that uses the power of waves to do acrobatic stunts.

Grab handle All canoes and kayaks should have a grab handle for ease of lifting – and for something to clip onto if they have to be fished out of the water.

Grade Whitewater rivers are graded from 1 to 6. Some rivers vary in grade, and you may choose to walk around difficult sections.

Habitat An area or natural environment in which an animal usually lives.

Helmet Protective headgear, with a tough outer surface and inner padding. A helmet must fit correctly and have a secure strap.

Hull The underside of a canoe or kayak.

J-stroke A key stroke for canoeists, particularly solo paddlers, which combines forward propulsion and ruddering.

Karabiner A heavy-duty metal clip that is used to hold kit to a strap inside boats or to clip ropes to boats for rescues.

Knife A rescue knife should be part of the kit of any canoeing group so that ropes can be cut in an emergency. Young paddlers should take an instructor's advice before purchasing or using knives.

Land To bring a boat back to shore.

Launch To set out in a boat.

Paddle A single- or double-bladed tool, used to propel a boat through the water by a forward-facing paddler. By contrast, rowers face backwards and use an oar.

Roll The manoeuvre of righting a capsized boat. Kayakers can self-right their craft, and there are several styles of this 'Eskimo roll'.

Rudder An adjustable device jutting into the water from the stern of a boat to affect the direction of travel. A paddle can also be trailed to rudder a boat.

Ruddering Using the rudder to steer the boat.

Shaft The 'stick' part of a paddle.

Slalom A slalom canoe race involves a paddler taking his or her boat through a series of 'gates' in the required direction (upstream or downstream). Slalom is an Olympic discipline.

Spraydeck An apron-like piece of kit worn around a kayaker's waist, while its outer edge fits tightly round the rim of the kayak's cockpit. It must have an undamaged grab-loop for easy removal. This is also called a sprayskirt.

Stern The back of a boat.

Sweep An arc-shaped stroke used for turning.

Tandem boat A boat for a pair of paddlers. There are both tandem kayaks and tandem canoes.

Throwline A length of non-absorbant rope, usually kept in a bag. The rescuer can throw the bag to a paddler who has exited his or her boat and, by keeping hold of the other end, pull him or her to safety.

Trim The balance of a boat along its length. Weight in the bow or stern will change the trim.

Upstream Against the flow of a river.

Weil's disease An infection that canoeists or kayakers may pick up from any water source. It is serious but rare.

Whitewater Water that foams white around rocks and other obstacles and at the bottom of drops.

Further information

Books to read

Adventures Outdoors: Let's Go Canoeing and Kayaking Susanne Slade, PowerKids Press (2007)

Kayaking: A Beginner's Guide Nigel Foster, John Wiley and Sons (1999)

Kayaking and Canoeing for Beginners Bill Mattos, Southwater, (2004)

Kayaking, Canoeing, Rowing and Yachting Christin Ditchfield, Children's Press (2000)

Radical Sports: Canoeing Phil Revel, Heinemann Library (2000)

Useful contacts

Amercian Canoeing Association
www.americancanoe.org

Australian Canoeing (AC)
www.canoe.org.au

British Canoe Union (BCU)
www.bcu.org.uk

New Zealand Recreational Canoeing Association
http://rivers.org.nz/

In Britain, the Adventure Activities Licensing Authority (AALA) has a database of activity centres that meet its standards of quality and safety. It is important to learn canoeing from a qualified and regulated instructor.
www.aala.org

Websites

This website is packed with all the information you will need on canoeing and other paddle sports:
www.canoeing.com/

The BCU has its own quarterly magazine for members, called Canoe Focus. Log on to it at:
www.canoefocus.co.uk

Paddles is a newsstand magazine for enthusiasts of all the canoeing disciplines. You can find it at:
www.paddles.co.uk

The virtual sports library has links to many canoeing and paddling sites and offers a wealth of information:
http://sportsvl.com/water/canoeing.htm

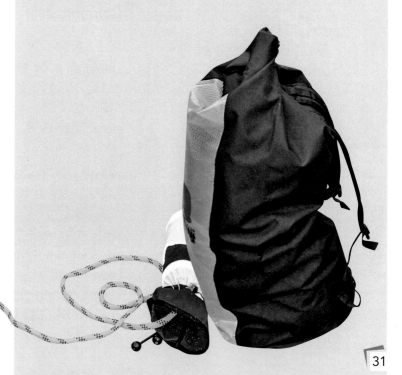

Index